DATE DUE

JAN 6 — 1970			
OCT. 7 1980			
NOV 28 1980			
JUL. 26 1982			
JUL. 22 1983			
JAN. 18 1984			
FEB 22 1985			
DE 19 '85	AP 10 '23		
MR 29 '89			
JAN 05 '96			
APR 08 '9			
MR 03 '06			
JE 15 '?			

11,540

Reinfeld, Fred, 1910-1964
    Chess for children; with moves and positions
pictured in photograph and diagram.   N.Y.,
Sterling, [1958]
    61p.   illus.,diagms

1.Chess.   I.Title.

CHESS
for
CHILDREN

with moves and positions pictured in photo and diagram

By
FRED
REINFELD

world-famous chess writer and champion player

STERLING PUBLISHING CO., INC.
New York

Contents

The photograph on the title page shows how, by giving check with the Queen, White forces the win of the Black Queen.

Thirteenth Printing, 1973
Copyright © 1958 by
Sterling Publishing Co., Inc.
419 Park Avenue South, New York, N.Y. 10016
Manufactured in the United States of America
All rights reserved
Library of Congress Catalog Card No.: 58-7612
ISBN 0–8069–4904–X
4905–8

1. Why Play Chess?

Chess is our oldest and most popular game. It is played in every country in the world by people of all ages. Despite the fact that the game is so old, more and more people are turning to it as time goes on.

There are good reasons for the great popularity of chess. In the first place, the chess pieces themselves are so colorful and varied that they fascinate even those who know nothing about the game. The shapes of the Rook and Knight, for instance, make you curious to know how these pieces move and what they can do.

Each of these pieces has its own distinctive way of moving and capturing. This is one of the things that makes chess the thrilling struggle it is. No other game can equal chess for excitement, for constant surprises, for unexpected turns of play that leave you breathless with amazement.

There is always something new in chess. It is not like other games, which are so limited in their possibilities that you soon lose interest in them. Just think of it! There are no less than 169,518,829,100,544,-000,000,000,000,000 ways to play the first ten moves of a game of chess!

Nevertheless, you don't have to know more than a few of these patterns to play well, and you don't have to be an expert to enjoy this wonderful game. You will always be able to find opponents on your own level of playing strength. Because your fascination

3

with chess will actually increase the more you play it, the game will give you a lifelong hobby. And, aside from the pleasure of playing, chess offers you many opportunities to meet interesting people and make new friends.

You may have heard that chess is most suitable for older people. This is far from the case. Chess is famous for its many child prodigies. Today, many schools in the United States, Canada and Great Britain have chess clubs and chess teams. Junior Championship tournaments attract skilled youngsters who often graduate into the ranks of experts. In fact, young people have distinguished themselves in tournament and match competition with the great masters of their time.

George Kramer, for example, won the New York State Championship several years ago from a strong field at the age of 16. More recently, William Lombardy duplicated this feat at the same age. In England, young Jonathan Penrose has held his own in tournament play against world-famous masters.

Among the child prodigies was José Raoul Capablanca, who learned to play at the age of 4 by watching his father at a chessboard with a family friend. At the second session, the little boy nearly earned a spanking by showing his father that he didn't know how to move his Knights properly! In time this phenomenally gifted player became World Champion.

Paul Morphy, the greatest player ever produced in the United States, was beating the finest players of his time (the 1840's and 1850's) when he was so young that he had to sit on several fat books in order to see over the chessboard. Sammy Reshevsky, another famous child prodigy, gave exhibitions of his

chess prowess all over Europe and the United States, playing 25 or more grown-up opponents at the same time—and beating all of them with ease!

Reshevsky, in turn, had to bow to a new prodigy in the 1958 United States Championship, when he lost his title to 14-year-old Bobby Fischer. So, as these lines are written, the current United States Champion is 14 years old!

But, as I have pointed out, you don't have to be an expert to enjoy playing chess. It has something to offer to every grade of player.

It is more than merely a pleasant way to spend spare time. For chess is a struggle that reflects the problems of making a living when you grow up. It calls for many of the same qualities: alertness in taking advantage of opportunities; foresight rather than hasty, impulsive action; patience in difficult situations; determination in bringing a game to a successful conclusion.

Finally, a word of caution. Never allow yourself to become so absorbed in chess that you neglect your schoolwork. Observe this caution, and you will get the greatest pleasure and benefit from the finest game devised by the brain of man.

2. How the Chess Pieces Move and Capture

Each game has its special rules which you must know thoroughly in order to play properly. In chess, you can think of the two players as generals, each one in command of his own army. Just as an army has privates, corporals, sergeants, lieutenants, captains, majors, colonels, and so on, the chess forces at your command differ in their appearance, names and powers.

Each player has 16 pieces at the beginning of the game. The pieces on one side are light-colored, and are known as WHITE. The opposing pieces are dark-colored, and are known as BLACK. In books, these pieces are represented in diagrams by standard symbols. These symbols show you the make-up of the two opposing armies:

	one KING	
	one QUEEN	
	two ROOKS	
	two BISHOPS	
	two KNIGHTS	
	eight PAWNS	

(*Note*: ROOKS are the same as CASTLES, a term with which you may be familiar. But if you want to sound like an experienced chessplayer, always use the name ROOK.)

Now, what sort of battlefield do you set up these armies on? Diagram 1 shows how the pieces are placed at the start of a game. In this diagram, as in all chess diagrams, imagine the player of the White pieces sitting at the near or bottom end of the diagram; the player of the Black pieces is at the far or top end of the diagram.

The chessboard is made up of 64 squares arranged in 8 rows. These squares are alternately "white" (light-colored) and "black" (dark-colored).

Note that the right-hand corner square nearest each player is always a white square. This applies to chess diagrams and also to the way the chessboard must be placed between the players.

Diagram 1

BLACK

WHITE

The opening position in a game of chess

Photo 1

THE OPENING POSITION

The board is always placed so that the right-hand corner square nearest each player is a white square. Compare the photographed chessmen with the symbols for them in the diagram above.

7

King's crown

Queen's crown

Rook

Bishop

Knight

Pawn

Now, to set up your chess pieces in the position of Diagram 1, you need a brief description of the pieces.

The King (see left) is always the tallest piece. It has a crown, which is generally topped by a cross. Each player has one King.

The Queen (see right) is the next tallest piece. It also has a crown, generally with small notches. Each player has one Queen.

The Rook (see left) looks like a tower or a castle. Each player has two Rooks.

The Knight is topped with a horse's head, reminding us of the days when knights fought on horseback. Each player has two Knights.

The Bishop, with a slit on top, gets its name from its resemblance to a bishop's hat, known as a miter. Each player has two Bishops.

The Pawn, the smallest of the chess forces, has a ball on top. Each player has eight Pawns.

In setting out the pieces in the opening position, compare each piece to the descriptions just given. Then study the position of the symbols in Diagram 1 before placing the pieces on your board.

You will note that each player places his King, Queen, Bishops, Knights, and Rooks on the row nearest him. Such a row of squares, extending from left to right, is called a RANK.

Place the two White Rooks first in the two corner squares on White's side of the board. Then place the two Black Rooks in the two corner squares on Black's side of the board.

Next, place the two White Knights next to the two White Rooks, as in the position of Diagram 1. Do

Back Rank

8

File

White Queen on white square

the same for the Black Knights. Note that the White Rooks face the Black Rooks across the board. (A row of squares running from one player to the other is known as a FILE.) Likewise, the White Knights face the Black Knights (on the Knights' files).

Place the White Bishops and Black Bishops on your board in the position of Diagram 1. These also face each other (on the Bishops' files).

Now take the White King—remember, this is the largest White piece—and place it on the empty *black* square on the rank with the other White pieces.

Place the Black King in the same row with the other Black pieces on the empty *white* square. The two Kings should face each other on the King file.

Now place the White Queen on the remaining empty (white) square on White's first rank. Then place the Black Queen on the remaining empty (black) square on Black's first rank.

To make sure you have placed the pieces correctly, check with the position in Diagram 1. Each player's back row, or rank, should now be filled completely.

Remember the useful rule of "Queen on its own color." The White Queen goes on a white square, the Black Queen goes on a black square.

Black Queen on black square

Now set the eight White Pawns on the eight squares of White's second rank, the row directly in front of the White pieces you have already set up. Then set out the Black Pawns on Black's second rank, directly in front of the Black pieces on Black's back rank. Check the position with Diagram 1, and you are ready to play.

In chess, White always makes the first move. Then Black makes *his* first move, and the players continue to move in turn.

King

Diagram 2

But before you can play, you have to learn how each piece moves and captures.

The King

The King moves one square at a time in any direction. It can move sideways, forward, backward or diagonally. (A diagonal is a row of squares of the same color which are joined to each other at the corners.)

In Diagram 2, each cross indicates a possible square to which the White King can move. On any one move, however, the King can travel in only one direction at a time.

The King can capture any opposing piece that occupies any square to which the King can move. For example, in Diagram 3 the White King can capture the Black Knight or either Black Pawn.

All chess captures are made in the same way: you remove the hostile piece as you capture it, and you replace it *on the same square* with the piece which is making the capture. No two pieces, friendly or unfriendly, can occupy the same square at the same time. Your own piece cannot be captured by your own man.

Remember, then, that in chess you capture by displacing the captured piece.

Diagram 3

The King cannot jump over hostile or friendly pieces. Since you cannot displace any of your own pieces, this explains why, in the position of Diagram 4, the White King cannot make any moves. (Incidentally, don't be puzzled by the absence of Black pieces in diagrams like this one. Many of the early diagrams in this book have been greatly simplified in order to emphasize a single point.)

Compare the situation in Diagram 4, where the King has no moves, with Diagram 2, where the King can choose from eight possible moves.

The squares to which a piece can move are the squares it controls—the squares on which it can capture hostile pieces. Although the King's moving and capturing powers are not very great, it is the most important piece in the whole game! This is explained in the section beginning on page 22; at the present stage you need only remember that the King is all-important, and that it cannot make any move or capture that will expose it to attack by any hostile piece.

The Queen

The Queen is by far the strongest piece on the chessboard. Like the King, it moves sideways, forward or backward, or diagonally, but it can move any number of squares at one time. Diagram 5 shows the enormous range of control by the Queen, which can move to *any* of the squares marked with a cross. From this diagram you can see that the Queen has a choice of moving in eight different directions along any line of empty squares. But, on any single move it can move in only one direction, which you are free to choose.

In the position of Diagram 5, then, the Queen has a possible choice of no less than 27 different moves. Of course, the Queen cannot move to any square occupied by its own pieces, nor can it leap over its own pieces or enemy pieces.

The Queen's far-ranging moves are one of the chief reasons why chess is the exciting game that it is. It is not unusual for the Queen to swoop all the way across

Diagram 4

BLACK

WHITE

Queen

Diagram 5

BLACK

WHITE

Diagram 6

BLACK

WHITE

the board to remove a strong hostile piece from a threatening position.

This is possible because the Queen captures the same way it moves. It can displace and capture any hostile piece that is within its moving range. It can of course capture only one piece on any given move. In the position of Diagram 6, the White Queen can capture the Black Rook or the Black Knight or the Black Bishop or any of the Black Pawns.

The Rook

Next in strength after the Queen is the Rook. The Rook can move in straight lines sideways, forward and backward. On any one move it can go in any one direction of your choice, along as many empty squares as you wish.

Diagram 7

BLACK

WHITE

The Rook cannot displace any of its own pieces. It cannot leap over its own pieces or enemy pieces. In Diagram 7, the Rook can move to *any* of the squares marked with a cross.

The Rook, with its great straight-line control, captures the same way it moves: it can capture (by displacement) any hostile piece that is inside its moving range. The Rook, of course, can capture only one piece at a time.

Diagram 8

BLACK

WHITE

The White Rook can capture the Black Bishop in Diagram 8 (by moving sideways) or it can capture the Black Knight (by moving backwards). Note that the White Rook cannot capture the Black Pawn, which is outside its moving range; it cannot move diagonally; nor can it move in two directions on the same move.

12

The Bishop

The Bishop can move any number of squares at a time in only one direction on any one move but it can move only on diagonals—squares of the same color. In Diagram 9, the squares marked by crosses are all squares to which the Bishop has a choice of moving.

You see from Diagram 9 that the Bishop has great power and range along the diagonals.

The Bishop cannot displace any of its own pieces. Nor can it leap over its own pieces or hostile pieces. But the Bishop can capture any hostile pieces (by displacement) inside its moving range. For example, in Diagram 10 the White Bishop has a choice of capturing any one of the Black Pawns.

Bishop

Diagram 9

Diagram 10

Diagram 11

Diagram 12

The Knight

The way the Knight can leap around the chessboard gives rise to many of the surprises for which chess is famous. The Knight's powers differ from those of the other pieces. If you are alert to the differences, you will often score against an opponent who is less aware of the Knight's unusual powers.

One special quality of the Knight is that its move is *always of the same length*. In Diagram 11, the squares marked with crosses each indicate a possible move that can be made by the Knight.

What is the principle underlying these Knight moves? In Diagram 11, note that each move is of the same length. Observe also that in the diagram position the Knight moves from a black square and always lands on a white square. (If he starts from a white square, he will land on a black square.) Thus, a Knight always moves to a square of the opposite color.

Let's look at one of the Knight moves in slow motion.

You can see from Diagram 12, then, that this Knight has moved one square sideways and then two squares forward.

In Diagram 13 we have another example of a Knight move. Here the Knight moves backward one square and then two squares sideways.

Now, returning to Diagram 11, let's examine each Knight move. What do you find? That all the possible Knight moves come under one of these descriptions:

14

(a) one square to the left or right; then two squares forward or backward, or

(b) one square forward or backward; then two squares to the left or right.

These moves can also be described:

(c) two squares to the left or right; then one square forward or backward, or

(d) two squares forward or backward; then one square to the left or right.

Diagram 13

The result is always the L-shaped move which is the Knight's specialty.

A second way the Knight differs from the other pieces is that it *can* leap over its own pieces or hostile pieces. However, it cannot displace any of its own pieces, and it can capture only hostile pieces located on the final square it lands on. Diagram 14 shows how the Knight captures, and how it leaps over pieces.

The White Knight can capture either Black Pawn in the position of Diagram 14. It cannot capture the Black Rook, but it can leap over the Black Rook in making these captures.

In the position of Diagram 14, there are also four other possible moves that the Knight can make; all these other moves are to empty squares where no capture is achieved.

Later on, you'll find other ways in which the Knight uses its special powers (see page 26). Of course, the Knight is like the other pieces, too, in a number of respects. It can move to only one square at a time. It can make only one capture at a time, and it captures by displacement.

Diagram 14

15

The Pawn

Though the Pawn is the least powerful of all the chessmen, you cannot regard it lightly for it has certain qualities which add to its effectiveness and make chess more exciting. A thorough grasp of the special features of the Pawn will help you to become a good player.

The Pawn can move in only one direction: straight ahead. But it has a special way of capturing. Before going into this, let's give the Pawns their full names.

The illustration on this page shows you the opening position again with all the Pawns on their proper squares awaiting the beginning of the game. Each Pawn is named for the file (vertical row) on which it stands. The King Pawn, for example, stands on the King file, in front of the King. The Queen Pawn stands in front of the Queen, on the Queen file, etc.

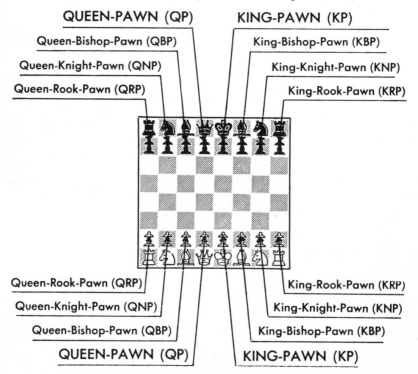

QUEEN-PAWN (QP)   KING-PAWN (KP)

Queen-Bishop-Pawn (QBP)   King-Bishop-Pawn (KBP)

Queen-Knight-Pawn (QNP)   King-Knight-Pawn (KNP)

Queen-Rook-Pawn (QRP)   King-Rook-Pawn (KRP)

Queen-Rook-Pawn (QRP)   King-Rook-Pawn (KRP)

Queen-Knight-Pawn (QNP)   King-Knight-Pawn (KNP)

Queen-Bishop-Pawn (QBP)   King-Bishop-Pawn (KBP)

QUEEN-PAWN (QP)   KING-PAWN (KP)

White Pawns always move toward the Black side. In diagrams, they move up the page.

Black Pawns always move toward the White side. In diagrams, they move down the page.

At *any* stage of the game, if a Pawn has not moved from its home square, its first move can be one square ahead *or* two squares ahead. But once a Pawn has left its original square, it can move ahead only one square at a time.

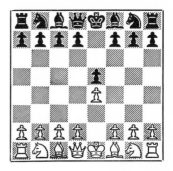

Diagram 15

Diagram 15 shows the position after White starts the game by advancing his King Pawn two squares and Black replies by advancing *his* King Pawn two squares. Now neither of these Pawns can move: they are blocking each other's way. Nor can either Pawn capture the other: their capturing method is different from anything you've seen so far.

The Pawn captures by taking the piece that occupies *either square diagonally ahead* of it. This means that it controls two squares. In Diagram 16 the White Pawn can capture the Black Knight *or* the Black Queen. It cannot capture the Black Pawn; nor can the Black Pawn capture the White Pawn.

Diagram 16

When the Pawn captures, it *displaces* the piece captured, the same way all other chessmen do. In Diagram 16, the Pawn would move to the next file left in capturing the Black Knight or to the next file right in capturing the Black Queen. When it captures, it assumes the name of the file it moves to. Thus, the Queen Pawn becomes the Queen Bishop Pawn if it takes the Knight here. If it takes the Queen, it becomes the King Pawn.

Diagram 17

Before King-side Castling

Diagram 18

After King-side Castling

You have already learned that the King is the most important piece in chess. You must therefore be very careful to shield your King as much as possible from enemy attacks and threats.

One of the best ways to guard your King is by means of a special move known as CASTLING.

Castling is the only move in chess in which you move two pieces at a time—your King and a Rook. This is still considered a single move.

Castling is also the only move that a player can make only once during a game. You can Castle *only if* there is a clear space in your back row between the pieces to be moved.

There are two ways to Castle. You can Castle King-side (with the King and the nearest Rook, called the "King Rook"); or you can Castle Queen-side (with the King and the further Rook, called the "Queen Rook").

Diagrams 17 and 18 show the situation before and after King-side Castling.

Here is how *White* carries out *King-side* Castling:

(1) Starting from the position of Diagram 17, he moves his King *two* squares to the right. (Note that there are no pieces in the way.)

(2) He places his King Rook at the immediate left of his King's new position. This is the situation in Diagram 18.

Here is how *Black* carries out *King-side* Castling:

(1) Starting from the position of Diagram 17, he moves his King *two* squares to the left.

(2) He places his King Rook at the immediate

Photo 2

White has just moved his King two squares to the right, and then picked up his King Rook from its original square. He is about to put the Rook on the square to the immediate left of his King. This will complete his Castling move.

Diagram 19

Before Queen-side Castling

right of his King's new position. This is the situation in Diagram 18.

Castling with the other Rook (the Queen Rook) is pictured in Diagrams 19 and 20.

Here is how *White* carries out *Queen-side* Castling:

(1) Starting from the position of Diagram 19, he moves his King *two* squares to the left.
(2) He places his Queen Rook at the immediate right of his King's new position. This is the situation in Diagram 20.

Here is how *Black* carries out *Queen-side* Castling:

(1) Starting from the position of Diagram 19, he moves his King two squares to the right.
(2) He places his Queen Rook at the immediate left of his King's new position. This is the situation in Diagram 20.

Diagram 20

After Queen-side Castling

19

Diagram 21

White cannot Castle because he has moved his King.

How does this protect the King? It helps to get your King into a safe place, usually protected by a wall of Pawns. It also gets your Rook into a position nearer the center of the board where it will be more useful. Therefore Castling is a valuable move and you want to Castle as early in the game as possible. Castling King-side is considered the safer of the two ways to Castle; so, *Castle early on the King-side.*

There are a number of cases in which it is not possible to Castle.

If you have moved your King, you cannot Castle later on. (See Diagram 21.)

If you have moved a Rook, you cannot Castle with that Rook. (See Diagram 22.)

If you have moved both Rooks, you cannot Castle at all.

There are several situations in which Castling is impossible for the time being; it *may* become possible later on.

For example, if your King is attacked (IN CHECK), you cannot Castle at that particular point. (See Diagram 23.) But you may be able to Castle later on.

Diagram 22

White can Castle King-side; he cannot Castle Queen-side.

Diagram 23

White cannot Castle at this point because his King is attacked by a Black Bishop. (White's King is in check.)

20

You cannot Castle if the square to which you want to move your King is commanded by an enemy piece. (See Diagram 24.) But you may be able to Castle later if this enemy control disappears.

You cannot Castle if a square that the King has to pass over is commanded by an enemy piece. (See Diagram 25.) But you may be able to Castle later, if this enemy control disappears.

As mentioned earlier, you cannot Castle if any of the squares between your King and the Rook to be Castled are occupied—either by your own or enemy pieces. (See Diagram 26.) However, you can Castle later on if the squares become empty.

A final note on Castling: the Rook can pass over, or land on, squares that are attacked by the enemy.

Diagram 24

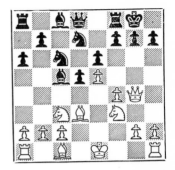

White cannot Castle at this point because the square on which his King would land is commanded by Black's black-square Bishop.

Diagram 25

Black can Castle Queen-side, but not King-side, where his King would have to pass over a square controlled by White's black-square Bishop.

Diagram 26

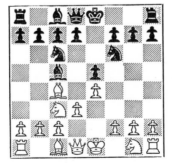

White is unable to Castle, as the squares between his King and Rooks are not empty. Black, on the other hand, is free to Castle King-side.

3. How to Win Chess Games

You win a game of chess by attacking the hostile King until he can no longer escape capture. When this final situation is reached, the King is said to be CHECKMATED. This ends the game. It does not matter how many pieces are left on the board.

Often a player who has a losing game will not wait to be checkmated. Instead, he admits defeat by surrendering at once; this is known as "resigning" the game. So, you win a game of chess when you checkmate your opponent's King, or when your opponent resigns.

Check

Diagram 27

Directly attacking the King is known as GIVING CHECK or CHECKING the King. Whenever the King is in check, he must immediately be taken out of check—out of the range or line of attack.

In order to have a clear understanding of check and checkmate, you must keep two points in mind:

(1) You can never move your King into check.

(2) You can never move any of your pieces in a way that would expose your King to check.

In Diagram 27 White's Queen is checking Black's King. Black's King, as you know, has to get out of check. There are three ways in which this can be done:

(1) Move the King to a square where he will no

longer be in check. (In Diagram 27, there are six possible King moves which will get the Black King out of check.)

(2) Interpose one of your Pawns or pieces in the line of attack. (In the position of Diagram 27, Black can interpose his Rook on the diagonal to stop the check.)

(3) Capture the hostile piece that is giving check. (In Diagram 27, Black applies this method by capturing the White Queen with his Pawn. Remember how the Pawn captures?)

Diagram 28

In the position of Diagram 28, White is checked by the Black Knight.

White cannot capture the Knight; nor can he interpose any of his pieces (because the Knight is the one piece that can leap right over anything). Lastly, White cannot move his King, for moving to either square that is open would put his King inside the capturing range of Black's Bishop.

The situation, then, is that White's King is in check and has no way of getting out of check. White is checkmated; the game is over; Black has won.

Note that when a King is checkmated, he is never captured or removed from the board. As long as the King is trapped with no chance of escape, the game ends right then and there.

Relative Values of the Chess Forces

Each man on the chessboard has a value. Since each piece's value is different, you have to know its worth in relation to other pieces so that you can avoid giving up a man of greater value for one of lesser value.

In addition, if you capture an enemy unit without losing one of your own, you have to know the value of the material you have gained. To be ahead in the value of your material, to outnumber your opponent's forces, is an advantage with which you can almost always enforce checkmate sooner or later.

The table of values shown here should be memorized; it will help you to know when you are sufficiently ahead in power to win by careful play.

QUEEN	9	points
ROOK	5	points
BISHOP	3	points
KNIGHT	3	points
PAWN	1	point

The King has no numerical value, as it cannot be removed from the board.

As Bishop and Knight have the same value, you may freely exchange one for the other. If you capture your opponent's Knight and lose your Bishop in return, you have made an even exchange.

To give up a Bishop or Knight (3 points) for a Pawn (1 point) is very bad play, and should eventually lose the game for you.

If, after an exchange of pieces, you have equal forces except that you have a Rook (5 points) when your opponent has just a Bishop or Knight (3 points), you are said to be THE EXCHANGE ahead. This is an advantage in material which should eventually win the game for you.

But material advantage is not all—you need a strong position, too.

Discovered Check

The usual way to give check is to move a piece or Pawn to a square from which it attacks your opponent's King.

In a DISCOVERED CHECK, however, you use a different method. In this case, you move a piece or Pawn that has been *blocking* a line of attack on the enemy King. When you move it out of the way, you let another piece, whose action has been blocked, proceed to "discover" check without having moved.

In Diagram 29, White can move his Pawn forward one square and let his Queen "discover" check.

Discovered checks generally come as a surprise, and sometimes they win valuable material.

In Diagram 30, White can give a discovered check by moving his Rook out of the diagonal row which his Bishop controls. If he's clever, he will kill two birds with one stone by moving his Rook three squares to the left, or one square backward. With either move, White not only gives discovered check but also attacks Black's Queen. As Black must move his King out of check (or interpose his Queen), he will lose his Queen on White's next move.

Diagram 29

Diagram 30

Photo 3

DISCOVERED CHECK

By moving his Rook, White will uncover his Bishop's diagonal, so the Bishop can give check. Such a move is called a *discovered check*.

Double Check

This is a special case of discovered check: the piece that uncovers check also gives check at the same time.

The only way to answer a double check is to move the King. Double checks are so powerful that they often force a quick victory.

Forking Checks

The Knight's power of attacking in two or more directions at the same time (called a FORK) makes it a powerful weapon. When the fork is combined with a check, the effect can be deadly. For the attacked King must move out of check, so that the other forked piece has no time to escape.

In Diagram 33 White's Knight forks Black's King and Queen with check. Black must move his King out of check. (There is no way of interposing a piece to break up a check by a Knight.) White then captures the Black Queen with his Knight.

Diagram 31

White can give discovered check by moving his Bishop.

Diagram 32

White is giving double check (with his Rook and also with his Bishop).

Diagram 33

Black to play

4. How to Read Chess Moves

Diagram 34

The opening position

To read chess moves, you need to know the exact name of each chessman and the name of each square. You will recall from the illustration on page 16 that each Pawn gets named right at the beginning of the game. This name comes from the piece in front of which the Pawn is placed.

Starting with the back row for both White and Black and moving from the extreme left in the opening position across to the right, here are the names and abbreviations used for the pieces and Pawns:

Names of the Pieces

QUEEN ROOK (QR)
QUEEN KNIGHT (QN)
QUEEN BISHOP (QB)
QUEEN (Q)
KING (K)
KING BISHOP (KB)
KING KNIGHT (KN)
KING ROOK (KR)

Names of the Pawns

QUEEN ROOK PAWN (QRP)
QUEEN KNIGHT PAWN (QNP)
QUEEN BISHOP PAWN (QBP)
QUEEN PAWN (QP)
KING PAWN (KP)
KING BISHOP PAWN (KBP)
KING KNIGHT PAWN (KNP)
KING ROOK PAWN (KRP)

If you play in a tournament, you have to keep a written score of your game as you make your moves. Even if you are not a tournament player, you may want to write down some of your games so that you can study the moves afterwards.

But the most important reason for learning how to record chess moves is to enable you to read chess

Diagram 35

This is the Queen file.

books and follow games played by the masters of chess. This will help you to become a much better player and will greatly increase your enjoyment of the game as you become familiar with its many fine points.

Names of the Squares

The board consists of FILES (vertical rows of squares) and RANKS (horizontal rows of squares). Each file is permanently named for the piece that stands on it at the beginning of the game.

Each player numbers the ranks from his side of the board:

Diagram 36

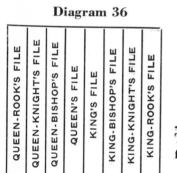

Diagram 37

This is a rank.
➡

⬅ The names of all the files.

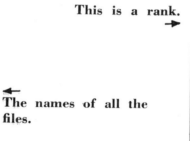

Diagram 38

8	WHITE'S EIGHTH RANK
7	
6	
5	
4	
3	
2	
1	WHITE'S FIRST RANK

The ranks numbered from White's side of the board.

Diagram 39

1	BLACK'S FIRST RANK
2	
3	
4	
5	
6	
7	
8	BLACK'S 8TH RANK

The ranks numbered from Black's side of the board.

28

By combining the names of the files and the numbers of the ranks, a name is given to each square on the board. Here is how all the squares are named:

Diagram 40

BLACK

QR8	QN8	QB8	Q8	K8	KB8	KN8	KR8
QR7	QN7	QB7	Q7	K7	KB7	KN7	KR7
QR6	QN6	QB6	Q6	K6	KB6	KN6	KR6
QR5	QN5	QB5	Q5	K5	KB5	KN5	KR5
QR4	QN4	QB4	Q4	K4	KB4	KN4	KR4
QR3	QN3	QB3	Q3	K3	KB3	KN3	KR3
QR2	QN2	QB2	Q2	K2	KB2	KN2	KR2
QR1	QN1	QB1	Q1	K1	KB1	KN1	KR1

WHITE

Because the ranks are numbered one way from White's side of the board, and another way from Black's side, each square has two names.

As you look at any given square, the name at the bottom is White's name for that square. The name printed upside down is Black's name for that same square.

When White makes a move to a given square, use the White name for that square. When Black makes a move, use the Black name for that square.

In writing down moves, use the abbreviated names of the pieces, Pawns and squares. The record of a move consists of the name of the piece or Pawn that makes the move, and the name of the square to which it moves. For instance, B—QB4: Bishop moves to Queen Bishop 4.

Here are some abbreviations that are commonly used:

moves to	—	piece at certain square	(P/B7)
captures	x	en passant	e.p.
Castles	o—o	(explained on page 35)	
(o—o—o, Queen side)		good move	!
check	ch	very good move	!!
discovered check	dis ch	bad move	?
double check	dbl ch	very bad move	??

Here are some examples of notation:

PxB: Pawn takes Bishop.

R—Q7ch: Rook moves to Queen 7 giving check.

N—KB6?: Knight to King Bishop 6. This is a bad move.

White's move always is stated first. Therefore, if you want to start with a move that Black has made, you put three dots before the move, such as 4 . . . P—K5; 5 Q—R5. This means that on Black's fourth move he advances his Pawn to King 5 and White replies on his fifth move with Queen to Rook 5.

The following brief sample game will give you practice in reading chess moves:

Diagram 41

WHITE	BLACK
1 P—K4	P—K4

This gives us the position shown in Diagram 15.

2 B—QB4	B—QB4
3 Q—KR5	N—QB3??
4 QxBP mate	

Mating position

30

Black's King cannot capture the White Queen, as this would put the Black King inside the capturing range of White's Bishop on Queen Bishop 4.

Note that White's second move would ordinarily be written B—B4. It is not necessary to specify *which* B4 in this case, as the Bishop can go only to Queen Bishop 4.

Similarly, it would have been good enough to write White's fourth move Q—R5.

However, Black's third move is a different story. To write N—B3 would have been confusing, because Black's Queen Knight could go to Queen Bishop 3, while his King Knight could go to King Bishop 3. Hence we write N—QB3 in this case to avoid confusion.

If two Knights can move to the same square from a given position, then you might name the Knight, as KN—QB3. Also if a piece can be taken by either of two Pawns, or if two Pawns are under attack, you might write: QBPxP/Q4, which means Queen Bishop Pawn takes the Pawn at Queen 4.

5. How to Force Checkmate

Diagram 42

Checkmate with the Queen.

Diagram 43

Checkmate with the Rook.

From the table of relative values (page 24) you learned what pieces to exchange so that you win more material than you give up in return.

Gaining material in an exchange gives you more attacking power than your opponent, and enables you to win still more material. Sooner or later, you will have an advantage in material so great that you can force checkmate no matter what your opponent does.

Sometimes, in order to win when you have a material advantage, you must try to make even exchanges just to clear the board. Then your advantage will be more firmly established. For instance, there are certain basic endgame positions for forcing checkmate against any resistance. You can aim for these positions when you have at least the following material advantages:

(1) King and Queen against King.
(2) King and Rook against King.
(3) King and two Bishops against King.
(4) King and Bishop and Knight against King.

In Diagrams 42 and 43, as well as in Diagrams 44 and 45, note that all the requirements for checkmate are fulfilled:

(1) The King is in check.
(2) The checking piece cannot be captured.
(3) It is impossible to interpose against the check.
(4) The King cannot move out of check.

It is important for you to be thoroughly familiar with these basic checkmate positions. Knowing them will enable you to win many endgames. Using this knowledge will prevent floundering in the middle game when you have a big advantage in material. You will seek to reduce your opponent's forces by even (or advantageous) exchanges until you are left with such an obviously superior force that your opponent resigns. If he does not, you can enforce checkmate.

Diagram 44

Checkmate with the two Bishops.

Photo 4

Diagram 45

Checkmate with Bishop and Knight.

CHECKMATE WITH THE TWO BISHOPS

This typical checkmating position reveals the great power of two cooperating Bishops. To win by this checkmate, you must force the hostile King into a corner.

6. Special Powers of the Pawn

Diagram 46

White advances his Pawn from seventh to eighth rank and replaces it with a new Queen.

Diagram 47

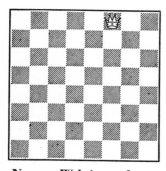

Now White has "queened" his Pawn which gives him an enormous material advantage.

You know from the table of values that the Pawn has the least value of any of the chessmen. For this reason the beginner attaches little importance to Pawns; he gives them away without a thought and rarely bothers to protect them.

But this is a mistake, for the Pawn has a power that raises its value enormously.

Pawn Promotion

When a Pawn advances all the way down to the eighth (last) rank, you must promote it to a Queen or Rook or Bishop or Knight. In almost all cases you will choose a new Queen, as that is the strongest piece on the board.

Your choice is not limited. For example, if you still have your original Queen, you can nevertheless acquire a new Queen by promotion, and have two Queens at the same time.

To QUEEN a Pawn successfully is the same as winning your opponent's Queen for nothing. You can therefore see that promoting a Pawn is one of the strongest moves in chess.

This will teach you to have more respect for the Pawns. You can never tell which Pawn may turn out later to be the one that becomes a new Queen.

Now, with your newly gained knowledge about the Pawn, you will see another way to win games. You already know you can win with a Queen ahead, but you can also win—most of the time—with only a Pawn ahead! For if you can turn this Pawn into a Queen, the result is such an enormous material advantage that checkmate can be forced.

There is still another way in which Pawns can be immensely important for winning purposes. If you come down to an ending of King and one Bishop against King—or King and one Knight against King —with no other forces left on the board, you cannot force checkmate.

But if you have a King and one Bishop (or Knight) plus a single Pawn against a lone King, you can win. You protect the advancing Pawn until it arrives at the eighth rank, and with the aid of the new Queen you force checkmate with ease.

Diagram 48

Capturing in Passing

The Pawn which has reached its fifth rank has a special power called CAPTURING IN PASSING. This enables it to capture in a way that is an exception to the general rule about Pawn captures (page 17). Only a Pawn can be taken in this type of capture. Let's look at the position in Diagram 48:

White's Pawn is on its fifth rank. As Black's Pawn is still on its original square, it can advance one square or two. If it advances *one* square, White can capture it if he wishes (leading to the position of Diagram 50).

But suppose that Black advances his Pawn two squares. Will he avoid capture?

No. On his next move only, White can capture the Black Pawn *as if it had advanced only one square.*

Diagram 49

35

Note that you can capture in passing only if you want to: you don't *have* to capture in passing.

However, if you are to make the capture, you must do it in reply to the two-square advance of the enemy Pawn. If you don't capture in passing on your reply move, then you lose your chance for good.

Diagram 50

White has captured the Black Pawn in passing, or "en passant" (e.p. in the abbreviated notation).

Photo 5

CAPTURING IN PASSING

Black has just advanced his Queen Pawn from his second rank to his fourth rank. *In reply*, White has captured Black's Queen Pawn in passing with his own King Pawn, which was on his fifth rank. White's capturing Pawn is now on the sixth square of the Queen file.

7. How Games Are Drawn

Most games of chess end in victory for one side and defeat for the other.

But this is not always the case. Occasionally a game ends with an indecisive result—neither side wins (particularly in championship games). Such a game is called a DRAW. In effect, the result is a tie.

Here are the ways in which a draw may come about:

Perpetual Check

This occurs when one player is able to force an endless series of checks without achieving checkmate or allowing his opponent to break the repetition of moves.

If you find yourself at a considerable disadvantage in a game, you will be glad to snatch at the opportunity to escape defeat by a perpetual check. This is effectively brought out in Diagram 51.

Black is a Rook down. Ordinarily this would be a crushing disadvantage, leading to certain defeat. But here Black is luckily able to save himself by getting a draw through perpetual check. This is what happens:

Diagram 51

WHITE	BLACK
1	Q—R6ch

White has only one reply to this check: he must interpose his Bishop.

| 2 B—R2 | Q—B8ch |

Again White must interpose his Bishop. Then we

have the position of Diagram 51, and the merry-go-round starts all over again.

| 3 | B—N1 | Q—R6ch |
| 4 | B—R2 | Q—B8ch |

Obviously there is no end to the checks. The game has to be given up as a draw. Thus Black has avoided defeat although he was a whole Rook down.

Draw by Stalemate

This is a drawing method that often works against careless players. To know how to use it, you have to be very clear about the difference between CHECK-MATE and STALEMATE.

In the case of checkmate (page 22) *the King is in check* and cannot get out of check. This means defeat for the checkmated player.

In the case of stalemate, your King is *not* in check; it is your turn to move; *whatever* you play, you would have to put your King inside the capturing range of an enemy piece, and this is not allowed by the laws of chess. Therefore, this is stalemate, and the game is a draw.

Black is a whole Queen to the good, and should normally win with ease. But whether he wins or not, depends on whose move it is!

If it is *Black's* move, he plays 1 . . . Q—KR1 mate. This is *checkmate*, because the White King is in check; the checking piece cannot be captured; no piece can be interposed to the check; and Black's King cannot move out of check.

Now go back to the position of Diagram 52. If it is *White's* move, he is *stalemated*, and the game is a draw!

Diagram 52

White's move, and he is stalemated. The game is a draw.

For if it is White's move:

(1) White's King is not in check.

(2) Every move available to him would put his King into check.

Hence, White is stalemated.

Another example of the stalemate idea appears in Diagram 53.

All of White's Pawns are blocked, so Pawn moves are out of the question.

White is not in check, but it is his turn to move and he has only moves that would put his King into check. Again this is a stalemate position; White has a draw despite his substantial material disadvantage.

Diagram 53

White to play

Draw by Insufficient Checkmating Material

Some games end in a draw because they come down to positions in which neither player has enough material to effect checkmate.

Diagram 54 illustrates one of these situations.

Obviously White's King can always escape to the black squares. Substitute a Black Knight for the Black Bishop in Diagram 54, and White's King is still safe. Checkmate is impossible; the position is a draw.

Other Types of Drawn Games

Draw by agreement occurs when both players agree to break off the game and call it a draw.

If fifty moves have been made on each side without a capture or a Pawn move, either player can claim a draw.

If a player is about to make a move that will repeat the same position for the third time, he can claim a draw.

Diagram 54

White to play

8. What to Do in the Opening

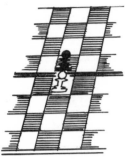

1 P—K4
P—K4

2 N—KB3

Playing the opening moves well is important, because your future prospects in a game depend on how you handle your forces in the opening. If you get a good start, you will have later opportunities for promising plans and powerful moves. If you play the opening badly, you will start off on the defensive, and all the winning chances will be on your opponent's side.

One basic rule to remember is to start the game by playing out the King Pawn two squares (1 P—K4) if you have White. If you have Black, answer 1 P—K4 by moving your King Pawn two squares (1 . . . P—K4).

By advancing this Pawn, you open up the diagonal of your King Bishop, so that you can bring out this piece quickly.

Another good idea is to bring out your King Knight early (N—KB3), perhaps on the second or third move, if that is possible.

By playing out these two pieces quickly, you will clear the two spaces between your King and King Rook, so that you can Castle early and get your King to a fairly safe spot.

Throughout the opening stage, consisting of about the first ten moves on both sides, concentrate on *bringing out as many pieces as possible*. These pieces—aside from the King—are useless to you while they remain on their home squares. Once you bring them

out ("develop" them), they will be ready for action—
to attack and threaten the enemy.

Avoid two beginner's faults that lead to trouble in
the opening. Don't keep moving the same piece con-
tinually; remember to develop new pieces all the
time. The other fault is to play a great many Pawn
moves, thus wasting time and creating weaknesses in
the early stages. Once you have played 1 P—K4, play
other Pawn moves sparingly. (The only other really
essential Pawn move will be an advance of the Queen
Pawn, to open the diagonal of your Queen Bishop.)

Some Standard Openings

As you study the game and become a better player,
you will find that there are standard ways of beginning a game. These standard methods have distinctive
names. Experts and specialists devote years of study
to these openings, but at the present stage you need
only be familiar in a general way with a few standard
openings.

GIUOCO PIANO

	WHITE	BLACK
1	P—K4	P—K4
2	N—KB3	N—QB3
3	B—B4	B—B4

The Italian name of this opening means "quiet
game," and that is just what it is. Since there is small
chance of difficult complications or dazzling surprises,
this is a good game for beginners. It continues:

Photo 6

GIUOCO PIANO

The usual position in this opening after Black's third move.
This is an opening recommended for beginners.

Diagram 55

Black to play

Position after White's 8th move

4	P—Q3	N—B3
5	N—B3	P—Q3
6	B—K3	B—N3
7	Q—Q2	B—K3
8	B—N3	. . . .

Black will now Castle and White will follow his example. The position is even as you enter the middle game.

42

SCOTCH GAME

Diagram 56

WHITE	BLACK
1 P—K4	P—K4
2 N—KB3	N—QB3
3 P—Q4	PxP
4 NxP	B—B4

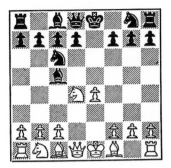

White to play

Position after Black's 4th move

White has opened up the game very rapidly and has a fine, free game for his pieces. But, since he has moved his Knight twice, he has lost time. Note that Black has played out two pieces, while White has developed only one.

In the position of Diagram 56, Black threatens to win a piece with . . . NxN or . . . BxN. So White protects his Knight by developing another piece.

5 B—K3	Q—B3

This attacks White's Knight again and once more threatens to win a piece. Again White defends the Knight some more.

6 P—QB3	KN—K2
7 N—B2	B—N3

The game is even at this point.

Photo 7

SCOTCH GAME

This is how the board looks after Black's fourth move. Black threatens to win a piece by capturing White's advanced Knight, which is attacked by two pieces and does not have enough protection.

Photo 8

FOUR KNIGHTS' GAME

This is the position after Black's fifth move. You see that both sides prepared early for King-side Castling, and have now Castled.

FOUR KNIGHTS' GAME

	WHITE	BLACK
1	P—K4	P—K4
2	N—KB3	N—QB3
3	N—B3	N—B3

Diagram 57

Black to play

Position after White's 7th move

This is the setup that gives the opening its name. Note how rapidly both players have brought out their Knights.

	WHITE	BLACK
4	B—N5	B—N5
5	Castles	Castles
6	P—Q3	P—Q3

Both players advance their Queen Pawns in order to make room for the development of the Queen Bishop.

| 7 | B—N5 | .... |

The position is even, though Black may find White's last move a bit troublesome to meet. This move "pins" Black's King Knight; this means that Black's King Knight is pinned to its square, for if it were to move, White could answer BxQ with an easy win. Such pinning moves are generally very strong because they limit the opponent's choice of moves and make him uncomfortable.

WHITE	BLACK
1 P—K4	P—K4
2 N—KB3	N—QB3
3 B—N5	....

Diagram 58

Black to play

This is the position from which the opening gets its name. It is one of the most popular and exciting of all the openings.

3 ....   P—QR3

Black is not afraid of the continuation 4 BxN, QPxB; 5 NxP. For in that case he regains the Pawn with 5 . . . Q—Q5, with double attack on White's King Pawn and advanced Knight.

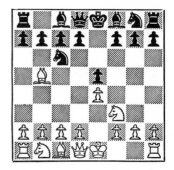

4 B—R4   N—B3

Position after White's 3rd move

Black continues with his development. He gains time by attacking White's King Pawn, and he is now ready to play . . . B—K2 followed by . . . Castles. An intensive struggle is in prospect.

Photo 9

RUY LOPEZ

Position after Black's fourth move. White is now ready to Castle King-side.

WHITE	BLACK
1 P—K4	P—K4
2 P—Q4	PxP

If White now plays the obvious reply 3 QxP, Black gains valuable time for bringing out his pieces by 3 ... N—QB3. This attacks White's Queen and forces him to lose time by retreating the Queen.

White thereby avoids this unfavorable line and decides on a totally different approach.

3 P—QB3	....

This move turns the opening into a "gambit"—a term which comes from an Italian word meaning to "trip up." A gambit is an opening in which a player gives away some material—usually a Pawn—in order to gain time for developing his pieces.

3	PxP

Black accepts the dare. Now White offers still another Pawn.

4 B—QB4	PxP
5 BxNP	....

Remember that the Pawn, as it captures, assumes the name of the file it moves to. Thus, the Pawn captured in Move 5 is the Knight Pawn.

White has given away two Pawns, but his long-ranging Bishops point menacingly at Black's position.

Both sides are taking risks. White hopes that he can crash through with a winning attack before Black gets his pieces out. Black hopes that he can develop

Diagram 59

Black to play

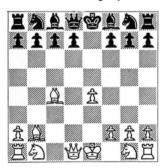

Position after White's 5th move

his pieces rapidly enough to hurl back any offensive that White can set up.

It is worth your while to play either side in gambits of this type. They always lead to exciting action and they give you good practice in learning how to attack and how to defend. Above all, they show you clearly how your chances of victory depend on the way you play the opening.

Photo 10

DANISH GAMBIT

Position after White's fifth move. The menacing attack of White's Bishops is what White was after with the "sacrifice" of two of his Pawns. Black will have to put up a stubborn defense to avoid disaster.

9. How to Win Quickly

People who don't play chess have an idea that a game takes a very long time. Actually, many games are over in jig time. If one of the players makes a bad mistake, his opponent can pounce on him and wind up the game with one or two powerful strokes. This is one of the features that makes chess such an exciting contest.

The following games will show some characteristic early mistakes which allow you or your opponent to win dramatically and quickly. You will find that you can apply all these ideas to win your own games in rapid order.

Diagram 60

White is checkmated.

1. "FOOL'S MATE"

WHITE	BLACK
1 P—KB3?	P—K4
2 P—KN4??	Q—R5 mate

White's foolish, weakening Pawn moves opened the gates to the enemy. This is the quickest checkmate you can bring off in a game.

2. "SCHOLAR'S MATE"

WHITE	BLACK
1 P—K4	P—K4
2 B—B4	B—B4
3 Q—R5	....

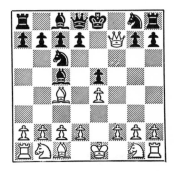

Diagram 61

White threatens QxKPch, but what is much more important, he also threatens QxBP mate.

Black sees the first threat, but overlooks the second threat.

    3 ....   N—QB3??

The right way was 3 . . . Q—K2, guarding his King Pawn *and* at the same time preventing the threatened mate.

    4 QxBP mate

Black is checkmated.

This mate is a good example of the suddenness with which a gross oversight in the opening can lead to a quick decision.

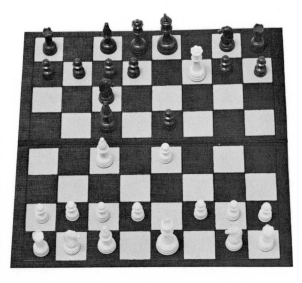

Photo 11

"SCHOLAR'S MATE"

A tried and true checkmating technique that has caught unwary victims for centuries.

3. PETROFF'S DEFENSE

WHITE	BLACK
1 P—K4	P—K4
2 N—KB3	N—KB3
3 NxP	N—B3

This is the idea: Black gives up a Pawn for quick development (his next move opens up the diagonal of his Queen Bishop).

4 NxN	QPxN
5 P—Q3	. . . .

White protects his King Pawn.

Diagram 62

5	B—QB4

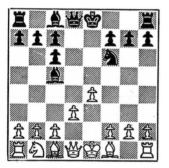

Position after Black's 5th move

While White has no pieces out, Black has developed two pieces and is ready for action.

White ought to play safe by continuing with 6 B—K2 and 7 Castles, protecting his King against the kind of danger that now turns up.

6 B—N5?	. . . .

White pins the Knight, under the impression that this piece cannot move because of the resulting loss of the Queen.

6	NxP!!

This is a "sacrifice." Black parts with his most valuable piece because he will obtain something more valuable in return: *Checkmate.*

7 BxQ	BxPch

50

This leaves White with only one possible move.

8 K—K2   B—N5 mate

White is checkmated, as his King is in check and cannot escape from check. Black was able to win in this startling fashion because White failed to take the proper measures to protect his King.

Diagram 63

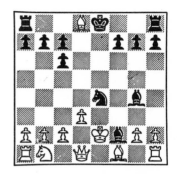

White is checkmated.

Photo 12

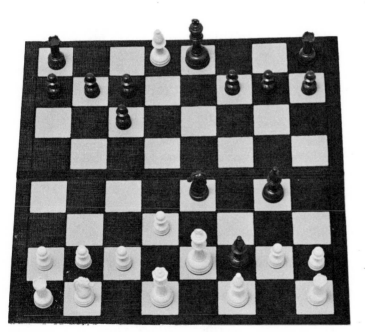

CHECKMATE!

After a clever "sacrifice" of his Queen, Black has quickly forced an excellent checkmate position. Brilliant possibilities of this kind are often overlooked, so watch for them!

51

4. GIUOCO PIANO

WHITE	BLACK
1 P—K4	P—K4
2 N—KB3	N—QB3
3 B—B4	B—B4
4 P—Q3	KN—K2?

This is a mistake. Black should have played 4 . . . N—B3, which is almost always the best way to develop the King Knight. In this case, 4 . . . N—B3 would have prevented White's later Q—R5, which comes in at the proper time with terrific power. But first:

5 N—N5	....

Double attack against Black's weak spot, his King Bishop 2 square. Note how the winner (in this case, White) hammers away repeatedly at this weak spot in these games.

5	Castles

Black brings his King Rook to the defense. But it is too late now for satisfactory defense.

6 Q—R5!	....

Still another attack (with the third piece) bearing on Black's menaced King Bishop Pawn—and in addition White threatens QxRP mate. Now you can see why Black should have played 4 . . . N—B3—to stop this invasion by White's Queen.

6	P—KR3
7 NxP	Q—K1?

Black can fight on longer with 7 . . . RxN, although

after 8 QxRch White is sure to win, as he is the Exchange and a Pawn ahead.

Diagram 64

8 NxRP dbl ch	K—R1
9 N—B7 dbl ch	K—N1
10 Q—R8 mate	

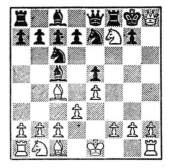

Black cannot capture the White Queen, as it is guarded by the White Knight; nor can he capture the White Knight, as it is protected by the White Bishop.

Black is checkmated.

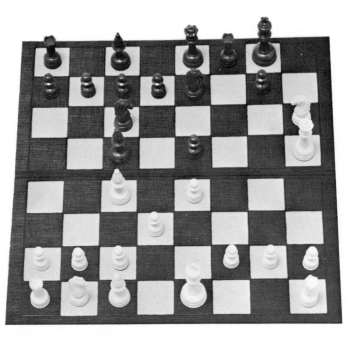

Photo 13

DOUBLE CHECK

This is the situation after White's eighth move. White is giving double check, with a Bishop and a Knight. Black's chances of escaping alive from such a check are very slight, as you can see.

5. QUEEN'S PAWN OPENING

WHITE	BLACK
1 P—Q4	N—KB3
2 N—Q2	P—K4

Black gives up a Pawn in the hope of confusing his opponent. Thanks to White's careless play, this plan succeeds.

3 PxP	N—N5

Diagram 65

White to play

Position after Black's 4th move

Trying to regain his Pawn.

But now all that White has to do is play 4 KN—B3, developing a new piece and protecting his extra Pawn. If White plays this he will be a Pawn ahead with much the better game. But he doesn't:

4 P—KR3??	....

This careless move ruins White's game at once.

4	N—K6!!

An amazing reply that forces victory.

If White does not capture the impertinent Knight now, he loses his Queen.

5 PxN	....

White has saved his Queen, but now he will be checkmated.

5	Q—R5ch
6 P—KN3	....

If White had not played 4 P—KR3?? this Pawn would now be protected and he would not be subject to checkmate.

54

Again and again this type of quick, decisive attack is used to punish players who commit serious mistakes in the opening.

Photo 14

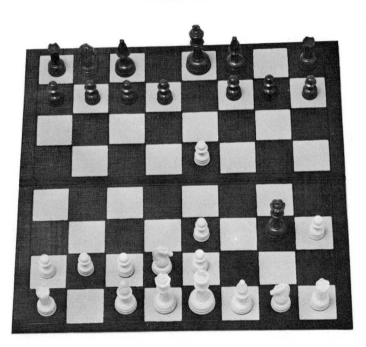

A MODERN "FOOL'S MATE"

This checkmate is based on the same idea as the ancient method shown on page 48. You can often apply a familiar attacking method to positions which are similar.

The next game shows you another murderous attack against a weak King Bishop 2 square.

55

6. PHILIDOR'S DEFENSE

WHITE	BLACK
1 P—K4	P—K4
2 N—KB3	P—Q3

This move guards Black's King Pawn, but it has the drawback of blocking the line of Black's King Bishop before it can be brought out. For this reason, 2 . . . N—QB3 (developing a piece) would be preferable, giving the same protection.

3 B—B4	B—N5
4 N—B3	P—KR3??

Black has only one piece developed, while White has three pieces in play. Almost any developing move (instead of 4 . . . P—KR3??) would have left Black with a safe position—for example 4 . . . N—KB3 or 4 . . . N—QB3 or 4 . . . B—K2.

But after 4 . . . P—KR3?? White has a startling reply.

5 NxP!!	. . . .

Diagram 66

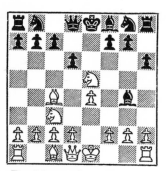

Position after White's 5th move

White's last move looks like a terrible oversight, as it permits the loss of his Queen. Actually, as in Game 3, this is a "sacrifice," and White gets good value for his Queen.

5	BxQ?

If Black had seen what was coming, he would have played 5 . . . PxN, allowing 6 QxB. In that case White, with a Pawn up, should win; but Black would still have some fight left. However:

6 BxPch	K—K2

7 N—Q5 mate

Again a player has been punished for making thoughtless Pawn moves.

Diagram 67

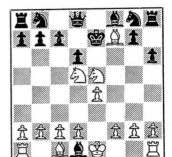

Black is checkmated.

Photo 15

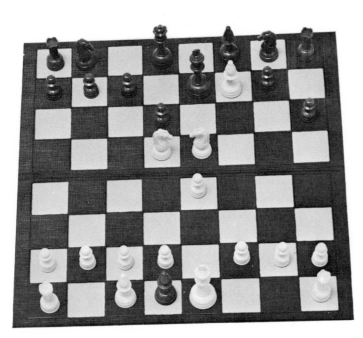

ANOTHER CHECKMATE!

Here again an early Queen sacrifice (this time by White) has led to an exciting checkmate position. Black's great material advantage is meaningless here.

Our final game illustrates another kind of mistake, and another type of punishment.

7. THREE KNIGHTS' GAME

WHITE	BLACK
1 P—K4	P—K4
2 N—KB3	N—QB3
3 N—B3	B—B4
4 NxP	....

This looks like a mistake, but the loss of material is only temporary.

4	NxN
5 P—Q4	Q—K2?

A mistake. Here Black's Queen is immediately exposed to attack.

6 N—Q5!	Q—Q3
7 PxB	....

Gaining more time by attacking Black's Queen.

7	QxP

And Black's Queen is still exposed to attack.

8 B—KB4	P—Q3

Diagram 68

White to play

Position after Black's 9th move

Black acts to protect his attacked Knight, which could not move because that would allow White to reply 9 NxPch—a forking check which would win Black's Queen Rook.

9 P—QN4!	....

This move leads to the forced win of Black's Queen.

9	Q—B3

58

The only move which does not lose the Queen at once.

        10 B—QN5!!   ....

Pinning Black's Queen, which cannot run away since it is on the same diagonal with Black's King. (Remember, you cannot expose your King to check.)

      10 ....   QxB
      11 NxPch   Resigns

Black surrenders, because after this three-way fork he must move his King out of check, and White continues 12 NxQ. This loss of the Queen would leave Black with a hopeless shortage of material, so he prefers to resign at once.

FORKING CHECK

This is after White's eleventh move. It is one of the deadliest moves on the chessboard. White gives check with his Knight, which at the same time forks Black's Queen—and one of his Rooks for good measure!

In these games you have seen typical mistakes in the opening which give you an opportunity to win quickly. As you study the moves carefully, you will become acquainted with many winning ideas and plans of attack which you can use in your own contests. They will make you a better and stronger player, and at the same time they will gradually open up your eyes to the many, many possibilities in each game of chess.

In this book you have learned all that you need to know in order to play chess. You can now go on to apply that knowledge in a number of ways. You can teach the game to your friends or family, and in this way you will have many happy, exciting hours at the chessboard.

Or, if you wish, you can join your school chess club where you will find keener opposition. If you become a good enough player, you will be able to match your wits with players from other schools in team matches and individual championships.

You may feel the urge to learn more about chess, to become a chess student and a stronger player, to enjoy going over the beautiful games played by great masters. Or you may go on to solving chess problems, which will challenge your skill and force you to think in new ways. Once you start to solve a chess problem, you will not be able to turn away from it until you have found the one perfect solution that completely clears up the mystery.

Perhaps you are unable to find any chess opponents. In that case you can still get a great deal of pleasure by reading chess books and learning more about the many beautiful sacrifices and combinations that give you the joy of discovery over and over again.

Some people play chess by mail, sending the moves on post cards. There are organized groups of "postal chess" players, which you can reach through chess magazines.

The wonderful thing about chess is that there is always something new to be learned, to be enjoyed, to be used "the next time." That is why chess never loses its hold over chessplayers. It offers just as much pleasure as playing a musical instrument—but without all the drudgery. So whether you become an expert or play just for the fun of it, you will want to come back again and again to your chessboard.